weblinks

You don't need a computer to use this book. But, for readers who do have access to the Internet, the book provides links to recommended websites which offer additional information and resources on the subject.

You will find weblinks boxes like this on some pages of the book.

weblinks

For more information about saving energy, go to www.waylinks.co.uk/series/improving/energy

waylinks.co.uk

To help you find the recommended websites easily and quickly, weblinks are provided on our own website, **waylinks.co.uk.** These take you straight to the relevant websites and save you typing in the Internet address yourself.

Internet safety

↗ Never give out personal details, which include: your name, address, school, telephone number, email address, password and mobile number.

↗ Do not respond to messages which make you feel uncomfortable – tell an adult.

↗ Do not arrange to meet in person someone you have met on the Internet.

↗ Never send your picture or anything else to an online friend without a parent's or teacher's permission.

↗ If you see anything that worries you, tell an adult.

A note to adults
Internet use by children should be supervised. We recommend that you install filtering software which blocks unsuitable material.

Website content

The weblinks for this book are checked and updated regularly. However, because of the nature of the Internet, the content of a website may change at any time, or a website may close down without notice. While the Publishers regret any inconvenience this may cause readers, they cannot be responsible for the content of any website other than their own.

HODDER
Wayland

Saving Energy

Dr Jen Green

HODDER
Wayland

An imprint of Hodder Children's Books

Titles in this series:
Air Pollution
Saving Energy
Saving Water
Waste & Recycling

For more information on this series and other Hodder Wayland titles, go to
www.hodderwayland.co.uk

Series editor: Victoria Brooker
Editor: Margot Richardson
Designer: Fiona Webb
Artwork: Peter Bull

First published in 2005 by Hodder Wayland, an imprint of Hodder Children's Books
© Copyright Hodder Wayland 2005

British Library Cataloguing in Publication Data
Green, Jen
Saving energy. - (Improving our environment)
1. Energy conservation - Juvenile literature
2. Energy consumption - Juvenile literature
I. Title
333.7'916
ISBN 0 7502 4658 8

Printed and bound in China

The publishers would like to thank the following for permission to reproduce
their pictures: Corbis (Ted Spiegel) 16, (Jim Sugar) 19; Ecoscene Photo Library
(Rosemary Greenwood) 8, (Kieran Murray) 9, (Visual & Written) 10, (Phillip Colla)
25, (Bruce Harber) 27; Still Pictures (Jochen Tack) 5, (Ron Gilling) 6,
(Julio Etchart) 11, (Peter Frischmuth) 12, (Mark Edwards) 13, (Adrian Arbib) 14,
(Shehzad Nooran) 17, (Jean-Francois Mutzig) 20, (Klaus Andrews) 21,
(Mike Schroder) 22, (Jim Wark) 23, (J Vallespire/UNEP) 24, (Michel Coupard)
26; Hodder Wayland Photo Library title page, 4, (Gordon Clements) 15, (Christine
Osborne) 18, (Timothy Woodcock) 28, (Angela Hampton) 29.
Cover picture: Wind turbines in Altamont, California by Getty Images

The website addresses (URLs) included in this book were valid at the time of going
to press. However, because of the nature of the Internet, it is possible that some
addresses may have changed, or sites may have changed or closed down since
publication. While the authors and Publishers regret any inconvenience this may
cause the readers, no responsibility for any such changes can be accepted by either
the author or the Publisher.

Contents

Words in **bold like this**, or in *italic like this*, can be found in the glossary.

Energy for life

Energy is the power that makes things work. Energy comes in many different forms, from wind that fills a boat's sails to the *fuel* in a car's tank. Your muscles also contain energy that allows you to move.

Everything we do uses energy. You've used all kinds of energy since you got up this morning. After waking up, you may have switched on the light and used energy to hop out of bed to a room heated or cooled by energy. After washing in water that took energy to heat, you ate breakfast which provided you with energy to get you to school.

Animals and people move by using energy stored in their muscles. Machines run on energy from fuels. ▼

Using energy

Every day, we all use huge amounts of energy. As the number of people in the world increases, more and more energy will be used. However, some of the main energy sources are now getting scarce. Also, using these sources can cause **pollution**, which is harming the world around us. That's why everyone needs to learn to use energy carefully, and not waste it.

▲ Every day everyone uses energy for transport, lighting, heating and cooking. We take it for granted, but the huge use of energy is harming the world around us.

TRY THIS! **Energy diary**

Make an energy diary, recording all the ways you've used energy today. Machines from kettles and cookers to cars all use energy. So do the lights and the heating or air conditioning that keeps homes comfortable. Your food provides a different kind of energy which you need to keep going all day.

Energy sources

You may be surprised to hear that almost all energy on Earth originally came from the sun.

Energy from plants

Plants use the sun's energy to make their own food, in a process called **photosynthesis**. In turn, plants provide us with food energy. Trees use sunlight energy to grow thick, tall trunks. The wood provides fuel for heating and cooking. However, in some parts of the world so many trees have been cut down that firewood is now scarce.

In many regions, people still rely on wood to provide much of their energy. In some places, all the trees around villages have been cut down, so people have to walk a long way to fetch wood. ▼

Fossil fuels

weblinks
For more information about
types of energy go to
www.waylinks.co.uk/series/
improving/energy

Coal, oil and gas all contain stored energy from the sun.
They are called **fossil fuels**, because they are the remains of
plants and animals that lived millions of years ago and have
been preserved as **fossils**. These fuels provide the world with
our main source of power.

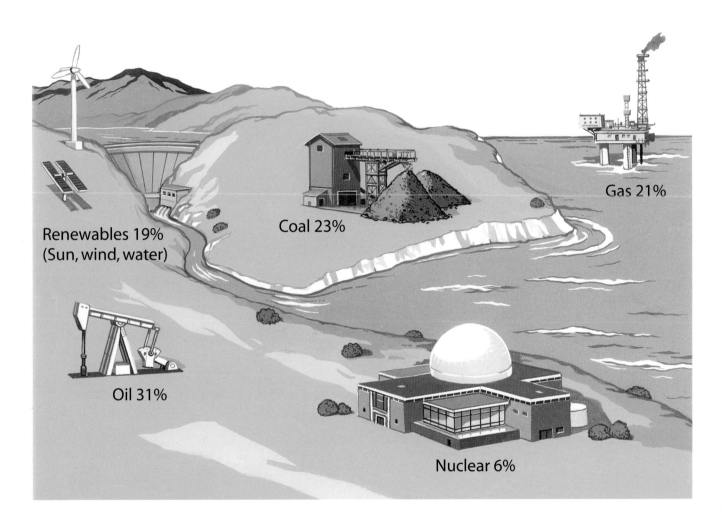

Renewables 19%
(Sun, wind, water)

Coal 23%

Gas 21%

Oil 31%

Nuclear 6%

Renewable sources

The sun, and other natural forces such as wind, flowing
water, and even hot rocks underground, can also be used
to provide energy. These are called **renewable energy**
sources because they are always being renewed by nature,
and will never run out.

▲ Fossil fuels provide
75 per cent of the world's
energy. Renewable sources
provide another 19 per cent,
while *nuclear power*
(see pages 20-21) provides
the remaining 6 per cent.

7

What are fossil fuels?

Fossil fuels were formed millions of years ago from the remains of plants and animals.

Coal

Black, shiny coal was formed from tree-like ferns that grew in swampy forests 300 million years ago. As the dead, fallen plants were buried under layers of soil, they were squashed and heated, and very slowly turned to coal.

Over millions of years, heat and pressure slowly turned the remains of giant tree ferns to brown, crumbly peat, and then to coal. This coal has been mined and is ready to burn. ▼

◄ Oil is mined on land, and also at sea by oil rigs that drill deep holes in the ocean bed.

weblinks▸

For more information about fossil fuels go to www.waylinks.co.uk/series/ improving/energy

Oil and gas

Oil and natural gas are the remains of **marine** animals and plants that got buried and squashed on the sea bed in a similar way to the coal-forming plants on land. Oil is now the world's most important energy source. We use millions of litres of it every single minute as we burn fuels made from it, such as petrol and **diesel**.

TRY THIS!

Energy at home

Make a list of all the energy sources in your home that provide power for heating, cooking, lighting and machinery. Do you use electricity, gas, oil, wood or coal? Any other fuels?

KNOW THE FACTS

Thick, black oil from the ground is processed in refineries to make many different products, including petrol and diesel for vehicles and fuel for aeroplanes. Oil is also used to make a wide range of other products found in homes, including clothes made from nylon and other *synthetic* fabrics, plastics of many different kinds and even paint.

Using fossil fuels

Fossil fuels are valuable. The companies that mine them are huge businesses. However, fossil fuels are a major cause of pollution.

When coal is mined, deep pits or underground tunnels are dug. Heaps of waste rock are left at the surface. Drilling for oil also causes pollution, and the giant oil rigs are hard to get rid of when they wear out. Fossil fuels are often mined in remote places, and have to be transported long distances. Tankers, pipelines and trucks carrying oil and other fuels can cause pollution if the fuel leaks out.

In 2002, the damaged oil tanker *Prestige* spilled 2 million gallons of oil into the sea near the north-west coast of Spain. The spilt oil formed an *oil slick* 8 km long, which was washed on to local rocks and beaches. ▼

◄ Traffic in Mexico City causes a poisonous haze called *smog*, which hides the hills surrounding the city and even the tops of tall buildings.

Burning

Power stations burn fossil fuels to **generate** electricity. Inside a modern plant, coal, oil or gas are burned to heat water to make steam, which spins machines called **turbines**. The turbines are connected to a **generator** that produces electricity. As fossil fuels are burned, huge quantities of smoke, **soot** and waste gases rise into the air.

Fuels for transport

Cars, lorries, planes and other vehicles consume huge amounts of fuel – about a third of all the oil used each year in the world. In the USA, vehicles use about half of the total oil used per year.

Energy use worldwide

In different parts of the world, people use very different amounts of energy. In *developed regions* such as North America, western Europe and Japan, we use far more energy than people in *developing regions* such as Africa.

Wealthy countries

Most people in developed countries use huge amounts of energy daily. Machines such as cars, vacuum cleaners and dishwashers make our lives comfortable, but guzzle fuel. Electricity is available at the flick of a switch. Developed nations have just one-quarter of the world's **population**, but consume a massive 70 per cent of the total energy.

▲ In richer parts of the world, lights blaze all night in shops and offices, which wastes energy.

Poorer countries

In developing parts of the world, there are fewer cars and other machines, so people use far less energy. Wood, animal dung or crop waste are often burned for heating and cooking instead of fossil fuels. However, the number of people in many developing countries is rising quickly, and people there also want the machines that make life comfortable. So, the use of fossil fuels is rising in developing countries too.

In developing countries when wood is scarce, people sometimes burn animal dung instead. This woman in India is drying dung to use as fuel. ▼

Running low

A hundred years ago, fossil fuels were cheap to produce and to buy, and it seemed as if they would last forever. Now we know stocks are limited, and will one day run out.

◄ Middle Eastern countries, including Saudia Arabia and Kuwait, hold the world's largest oil stocks. In the last 50 years, selling oil abroad has made these countries rich and powerful.

 **KNOW THE FACTS**

Scientists estimate that world stocks of oil and gas will only last for another 70 years or so. Coal stocks will last longer, for another few hundred years, but eventually they will run out too.

Non-renewable

Fossil fuels are called **non-renewable energy** sources, because once they are used up, they cannot be replaced. This is because coal, oil and gas took millions of years to form through processes that cannot be copied.

Burning oil

Every year, our use of fossil fuels increases, as more cars go on the road, more factories open, and more people buy fridges, cookers and other machines. If everyone used fossil fuels more carefully, there would be many more years before world stocks run out.

▲ In China, there are fewer cars than in developed countries. Many people walk or cycle to work rather than going by car.

Pollution problems

The growing scarcity of fossil fuels is not the only problem. The waste gases released as we burn these fuels are changing the world's climate, and also causing a problem called *acid rain*.

Acid rain

Vehicles, power plants and factories release polluting gases as they burn oil and coal. These gases mix with **water vapour** in the air to make rain that contains a weak acid. When acid rain falls, it harms trees and spills into rivers and lakes to kill water life.

A scientist takes a sample of the water at Woods Lake in New York state, USA, during the spring melt of snow. The lake has been badly affected by acid rain and scientists are trying to work out how much damage has been done. ▼

Climate change

Carbon dioxide and other gases in the air keep the Earth warm by trapping heat. This is called the **Greenhouse Effect**. When we burn fossil fuels, more carbon dioxide gets into the atmosphere. The extra gas is increasing the Greenhouse Effect and causing the Earth to overheat. This problem, called **global warming**, is causing **climate change**. Some dry areas are getting drier, others are getting wetter. The oceans are also warming up, causing them to expand, making sea levels rise. This means floods are more likely on islands and coasts.

▲ In recent years, the low-lying country of Bangladesh in Asia has been hit by terrible floods. Scientists fear floods like these are becoming more common because of global warming.

| weblinks |
For more information about acid rain go to www.waylinks.co.uk/series/improving/energy

TRY THIS! ### Explore the Greenhouse Effect

The Greenhouse Effect gets its name because the gases in the atmosphere act like the glass in a greenhouse, trapping heat inside. You can see how this works. Put a thermometer in a sunny place for ten minutes. Write down the temperature. Now put the thermometer in an air-filled, clear plastic bag. Seal the bag and put it in the same place for ten minutes. Is the temperature the same, or different?

Action on fossil fuels

Today the world faces an energy crisis because fossil fuels are running out and are also harming nature. People are taking action to try to reduce fossil fuel pollution and save energy.

Tackling the energy crisis

To solve the energy crisis, we all need to burn less fossil fuels. We can manage this both by using energy more carefully, and also by turning to other energy sources that don't pollute nature. Scientists can help by designing factories and machines that use fuel more efficiently and create less pollution. Governments can help by funding the development of renewable energy.

▲ Using buses, trains and other forms of public transport causes far less pollution than going by car. In Amsterdam, in the Netherlands, there is an efficient tram system that runs throughout the city.

Reducing vehicle pollution

Cars, trucks and other vehicles can also be designed to burn fuel more efficiently and give off less pollution. Some cars now run on solar power or electricity instead of petrol. Governments help by spending more on public transport, so people can use cars less, and also by building more cycle lanes, to encourage cyclists. In some cities (such as London and Singapore), drivers now have to pay a toll to enter city centres. This reduces the number of cars coming into cities, which helps to combat air pollution in built-up areas.

▲ A cyclist talks to the driver of a new type of car that runs on both electricity and petrol.

HELPING OUT Freeplay energy

Batteries that provide energy for radios and torches are made with chemicals that cause pollution when we throw them away. Batteries are also expensive. Now 'freeplay' radios and torches are available. They run on clockwork, and are powered by simply winding a spring. Buying products like these saves energy and cuts pollution.

Nuclear energy

Huge amounts of energy can be released by splitting atoms (tiny particles) of a rare fuel called uranium. This process, called nuclear fission, provides an alternative to fossil fuels, but there are drawbacks.

The first use of nuclear fission was to make bombs that caused great destruction during World War II (1939-45). Later, scientists discovered how to control the process to generate electricity. Nuclear fuels do not release the waste gases that are causing acid rain and global warming. However they do give off harmful **radiation** that kills living things, and so have to handled with great care.

Waste from the nuclear industry remains dangerous for thousands of years. No one has discovered a safe way to get rid of it, so much of it is just buried in sealed containers deep underground. ▼

▲ After the disaster at the Chernobyl nuclear plant, a huge clean-up operation was carried out. Workers had to protect themselves from radiation and from breathing contaminated air.

weblinks

For more information about nuclear energy go to www.waylinks.co.uk/series/improving/energy

A dangerous fuel?

In 1956, the world's first **nuclear reactor** opened in north-west Britain. Many people believed that nuclear energy offered an almost unlimited supply of safe, cheap power. Hundreds more nuclear power stations opened in the next thirty years. However, in 1986, the nuclear reactor at Chernobyl in Ukraine caught fire and exploded, showering deadly radiation over a vast area. Many countries have now turned away from nuclear energy because they think it's too dangerous.

KNOW THE FACTS

The accident at Chernobyl released a vast cloud of radiation that spread north, west and south in the following week. Around Chernobyl, 5000 sq km of land was declared unsafe, and everyone had to leave. Scientists estimate that up to 10,000 people have now died due to the radiation.

Energy from sun and water

The sun and flowing water contain energy that can be used to generate electricity. They cause much less harm to the environment than fossil fuels.

weblinks
For more information about solar energy go to www.waylinks.co.uk/series/improving/energy

Solar energy

The sun's energy can be captured in various ways. **Solar** panels trap heat which can then be used to heat water and houses, and even generate electricity. Solar power will not run out and causes no pollution, but it works best in sunny places. Although the panels and other solar technology are quite expensive to build, people save money by not paying for other types of fuel.

For solar panels to work efficiently, they must be angled towards the sun. This solar-powered house is in Germany. ▼

▲ When a dam is built, like this one in Utah, USA, the land behind floods to form a *reservoir*. Local people and even whole towns may have to move to make way for the dam.

Water power

Water flowing downhill contains energy. People have used this type of energy for thousands of years to drive machines such as mill wheels. This energy can be turned into electricity. Fast-flowing water spins turbines attached to machines called generators which change the energy into electricity. This is called **hydroelectric power (HEP)**. A dam is often built above the plant to control the flow of water. These huge dams change the landscape as an enormous lake, called a reservoir, is formed behind the dam wall.

23

Energy from wind and rocks

The power of the wind and also of hot rocks underground can also be used to generate electricity. These forms of energy are renewable and also 'clean', that is non-polluting. However like all energy sources, they have their limitations.

Geothermal energy

In volcanic regions, such as Iceland and New Zealand, hot rocks lie close to the Earth's surface. Cold water piped underground can be heated by the rocks to produce steam, which is used to make electricity. In most other countries, though, the hot rocks lie too deep for their **geothermal energy** to be tapped in this way.

▲ In Iceland hot rocks heat water to form hot springs. Geothermal power stations use the same heat to provide electricity.

▲ Wind farms are large collections of wind turbines.
This group in the USA provides power to the nearby town
of Palm Springs in California.

Wind energy

Old-fashioned windmills have been used for centuries.
Modern wind turbines are tall towers with propellers.
The wind spins the propellers, which are linked to electric
generators. However the turbines can only be sited in
windy areas, and some people say they are noisy and
spoil the view.

25

New energy sources

Scientists are working to develop new low-pollution energy sources. In future, we will probably rely on a wide range of ways to meet our energy needs.

Energy from the sea

Wave energy can be harnessed using large floating containers called 'ducks'. As the ducks rock with the waves, oil is pumped through turbines inside them to generate electricity.

Energy from sea **tides** can be captured by building a barrier called a **barrage** across a river mouth. Water trapped behind the barrage at high tide is released as the tide falls, to spin turbines. But tidal energy only produces one or two bursts of energy a day, because there are only one or two tides per day.

This tidal power plant on the River Rance in northern France has been generating electricity since the 1960s. The dam also doubles as a bridge. ▼

Energy for the future

Energy can be also generated by burning domestic rubbish in special **incinerators**. However their fires have to be kept super-hot, or poisonous gases escape. As well, scientists are working on a new kind of nuclear technology, called fusion, which uses **hydrogen** as fuel. In future, as fossil fuels run out, all these energy sources may become vital. But we also need to use less energy.

▲ A modern power station with a chimney designed to reduce the release of harmful gases.

HELPING OUT

Energy-saving bulbs

Energy-saving light bulbs are a bit more expensive than ordinary bulbs, but use just one-fifth of the electricity to produce the same light. They also last for much longer.

Taking part

We can all join in the efforts to save energy, which help to ease problems such as climate change. Young or old, if everyone does even a little, the total energy savings will be huge.

Saving energy is simple – just switch off lights, and machines such as TVs, radios and computers when you've finished using them. In cold weather, most energy used in homes goes on heating. Snug, well-**insulated** homes save energy. Warm air rises, so ask your parents to make sure the loft is well insulated. Seal draughty doors and windows. Put on a jumper and turn the heating down a couple of degrees!

◄ **Hanging out the washing in the sun, instead of using an electric dryer, is a useful way of saving energy.**

Cycle and recycle

Every family can make energy savings by using the car less, and other forms of transport more. Can you cycle, walk, or take the bus to school, or share a ride with someone in your class? Bottles, tins and other food and drink containers take a lot of energy to make. Take them to the local recycling centre instead of throwing them away.

weblinks

For more information about saving energy go to www.waylinks.co.uk/series/improving/energy

▲ **Try walking to the shops instead of driving. It's a good way to get some exercise – and saves money, too.**

HELPING OUT **Machines on standby**

Machines such as TVs, videos, radios and computers left on standby use up quite a lot of energy. If everyone switched them off, a lot of energy would be saved.

Glossary

Acid rain Rain which is extra-acidic because it is polluted by fumes from cars, factories and power stations.

Barrage A barrier built across a river.

Carbon dioxide A gas produced by burning, and by living things.

Climate change Changes in the Earth's climate take place naturally, but human activities are increasing the rate at which climate is changing. The burning of fossil fuels, which disturbs the natural balance of gases in the atmosphere, is mostly to blame. As a result, world temperatures are rising and in the future wild weather such as storms and flooding may become more common.

Developed regions The richer countries of the world, whose industries are well-developed. Developed countries include the USA, Canada, many European countries, Australia and Japan.

Developing regions The poorer areas of the world, whose industries are less well-developed. Developing nations include many countries in Africa, Asia and South America.

Diesel A fuel, like petrol, made from oil.

Fossil fuels Coal, oil, gas and other fuels formed from the fossilized remains of plants or animals that lived millions of years ago. Fossil fuels are currently the world's main energy source.

Fossils The ancient remains of plants or animals, embedded in rock.

Fuel Any material that can be burned to release energy, including wood and coal.

Generate To make or produce.

Generator A machine which produces electricity.

Geothermal energy Energy from hot rocks located underground.

Global warming Rising temperatures worldwide, caused by the increase of gases in the atmosphere that trap the sun's heat.

Greenhouse Effect The way carbon dioxide and other gases keep the Earth's surface warm. These gases act like glass in a greenhouse, trapping heat in the lower levels of the atmosphere.

Hydroelectric Power (HEP) Electricity generated from flowing water.

Hydrogen A gas that burns easily.

Incinerator An oven for burning rubbish.

Insulated Kept warm by a material which prevents heat from escaping.

Marine Belonging to the sea.

Non-renewable energy Energy that comes from sources that will run out, such as fossil fuels and uranium.

Nuclear power Energy released by splitting tiny particles, called atoms, of a fuel called uranium.

Nuclear reactor Part of a nuclear power plant where energy is made by splitting atoms.

Oil slick A thin layer of oil floating on water.

Photosynthesis The process by which plants make their own food using carbon dioxide gas, water, minerals and energy from sunlight.

Pollution Harmful or poisonous substances in the environment, such as in water or air.

Population All the things that live in a particular place.

Radiation Rays. Materials said to be radioactive give off dangerous rays.

Renewable energy Energy which comes from sources that will not run out, such as the sun, wind and flowing water.

Reservoir A large lake, either formed naturally or made by people, which is used as a water supply.

Smog Pollution in the air caused by motor vehicle fumes, sunshine and high temperatures.

Solar To do with the sun.

Soot Black powder released when coal or wood is burned.

Synthetic Something that is made by people; not natural.

Tides Rising and falling of the sea level.

Turbine A machine powered by steam, gas or water that is used to generate electricity.

Water vapour Tiny droplets of water in the air.

Further information

Reading

Earth Alert! Energy by Jane Featherstone (Hodder Wayland, 1998)

Energy Crisis by Jen Green (Chrysalis/Belitha, 2003)

Energy for Life series by Robert Snedden (Heinemann Library, 2002)

Living for the Future: Energy and Resources by Paul Brown (Franklin Watts, 1998)

Why Should I Save Energy? by Jen Green (Hodder Wayland, 2001)

Saving Energy Websites

http://www.eere.energy.gov/kids/
US Department of Energy: Energy Efficiency and Renewable Energy

http://www.rmi.org/sitepages/pid479.php
Rocky Mountain Institute for Kids

http://www.energyquest.ca.gov/index.html
California Energy Commission site for children

http://www.defra.gov.uk/environment/climate change/schools/index.htm
UK government site on global warming

Campaign Groups

Friends of the Earth
26-28 Underwood Street,
London N1 7JQ
Website: http://www.foe.co.uk

Greenpeace
Canonbury Villas,
London N1 2PN
Website: http:// www.greenpeace.org

WWF-UK
Panda House,
Weyside Park,
Godalming,
Surrey GU7 1XR
Website: http://www.wwf-uk.org

Index

Numbers in **bold** refer to illustrations.